BOSTON
The Way It Was

BOSTON
The Way It Was

Pictures and Memories
from the '30s and '40s

Lorie Conway

WITH A FOREWORD BY
Thomas O'Connor

WGBH Boston

Library of Congress Cataloging-in-Publication Data

Conway, Lorie, 1954–
    Boston: the way it was : pictures and memories from the Thirties and Forties / by Lorie Conway ; with a foreword by Thomas O'Connor.
        p.   cm.
    Includes index.
      1. Boston (Mass.)—Social life and customs—Pictorial works.
    2. Boston (Mass.)—Social life and customs.   I. Title.
F73.5.C758   1996
974.4'61042' 0222—dc20   96-27240
                                        CIP

Printed in the United States of America
First Printing

Preceding pages:

James Michael Curley throwing out the first ball on Opening Day at Fenway Park, 1922. Curley would dominate the Boston political scene for over thirty years.

The National Theatre, Tremont St., 1931.

Contents

JULES AARONS

Foreword

by Thomas O'Connor

The ferry *Nantasket*, c. 1930s, leaving from Rowes Wharf.

Ted Williams at Fenway Park, c. 1948. In a one-game playoff against the Cleveland Indians, the Red Sox lost their chance to play the Braves in the '48 World Series.

BOSTON is more than a geographic location. It is a way of life; indeed it is an experience that people who are born in Boston take with them wherever they go. It is always a part of them.

And there are certain periods of time in Boston's long and colorful history that people never forget, unique and memorable periods that usually separate one distinctive phase of life and society from another. They are periods that later generations inevitably look back upon with great fondness and nostalgia.

The nineteen thirties and nineteen forties were special decades in Boston's history. And there are still a great many people around who lived in the city during that era and can remember quite clearly what it was like. It was a peaceful time of family and friendship, when people of limited income and modest means could enjoy the simple pleasures of life and the intimacy of close-knit neighborhoods—communities like the West End, the North End, and the South End, where people of all races, creeds, and nationalities mingled. Families talked to each other from the back windows of three-decker houses, exchanged bowls of sugar for sticks of butter, handed down the clothing of older children for the younger children to wear.

These were years before television had appeared, and when people made their own entertainment. Family members gathered around radios in the evenings, or saved up enough money turning in milk bottles so they could attend double-feature movies at one of the elegant movie houses, such as the Metropolitan Theater, on the weekends. And after church on Sundays, families would pack up and go by streetcar to Revere Beach for an afternoon ocean swim and a ride on the roller coaster.

Boston sports teams were always popular attractions during the thirties and forties. The Red Sox played at Fenway Park, the Boston Braves offered reduced fees at Braves Field for young members of the "Knot Hole Gang," and Eddie Shore and the rest of the "Kraut Line" always brought fans into the Boston Garden.

Music was a big part of growing up during these decades. Orchestra leaders like Benny Goodman, Tommy Dorsey, and Harry James played to the enjoyment of young couples who loved dancing to the beat of the "Big Band" sound. Those who went into Boston could dine out at night-clubs like the Latin Quarter or the Cocoanut Grove. Those who had the chance to drive out to Auburndale could spend an evening dancing to America's top orchestras at the fabulous Totem Pole ballroom.

And then there was the legendary Scollay Square, an area of shooting galleries, tattoo parlors, and hot dog stands like Joe and Nemo's. It also featured stripteasers. Ann Corio pranced at the Old Howard, Sally Rand waved her feathered fans, and Sally Keith twirled her famous tassels at the Crawford House.

In many ways, the coming of World War II marked the beginning of the end of those "good old days." When the young men went off to war, ties were broken and that "old gang of mine" was never the same.

Despite all the changes and the new technologies, however, Bostonians still like to remember the way everybody knew one another, helped one another, worked together, built a life in common. Everyone was different, of course. People clung to their own ways, cooked their own foods, played their own music, dressed in their own styles, followed their own customs. But at the same time they found ways to enjoy their families and get along with their neighbors.

After all, that was Boston—that's the way it WAS!

Washington St., c. 1925. "Moving pictures" were the rage by the mid-1920s.

Eddie Shore, c. 1940. Known as the "Edmonton Express" because of his fierce speed and intense checking, Shore would help the Bruins win two Stanley Cups during the era.

JULES AARONS

Jules Aarons, c. 1950. Besides taking still photography of Boston's neighborhoods, Aarons made a film in the West End with an actual cast and residents used as extras.

Leslie Jones, c. 1940, gets on the other side of the camera for this *Herald Traveler* publicity photo.

Preface

*I*N 1981 I moved to Boston to work for WBZ television. Looking out over the city from my hotel room, I was amazed at what seemed to be an accessible "big city." At the time Boston was the sixth largest television market in the country, yet it had the look and feel of something much smaller. Here was a city with a walkable downtown with families living in it, and a riverway designed to be used: if you chose to live downtown, it was right out your front door. The decision was made. Wincing at the high rent but wanting to be in the heart of it all, I set up house, albeit on a small scale, in Boston's Back Bay.

After unloading the moving van, I put on my running shoes and headed for the river. Since then I've completed seven Boston Marathons, produced TV for three commercial television stations, received a Nieman Fellowship, Class of '94, and lived in a half dozen apartments, all within a three-block radius. I may not be a real Bostonian, because I wasn't born here, but this "little big town," as Mike Barnicle likes to call it, sure feels like home. And now that I have a son, I know he's a native: Max can flag down a cab much faster than I can. He also knows something about Boston history; going to school around the corner from Paul Revere's house makes the city's past a bit more real.

Producing the "Boston: The Way It Was" series for WGBH seemed like a natural for me. Having done countless stories on Boston issues, current and past, I felt I knew the city quite well. But once I began to research the era we were concentrating on, I realized that the Boston of fifty years ago was a very different place from the city I know. In 1930 the

Custom House Tower was the tallest building in Boston. Clubs stayed open till 3:00 A.M. Tattoo parlors, burlesque shows, a mayor serving jail time while in office, ballplayers who ate Tootsie Rolls thrown to them by fans, Count Basie jamming at the Hi-Hat? No way, I thought, not in this tame little city, where today it's hard to find a cup of coffee after 2:00 A.M.!

But then the photographs began to tell the story. With the superb assistance of Aaron Schmidt (and the blessing of Curator Sinclair Hitchings) at the Boston Public Library, I started to sift through hundreds of images taken by the renowned *Herald Traveler* photojournalist Leslie Jones. A small man, he wandered the city for over four decades in his trademark two-sizes-too-big overcoat and woolen cap. From 1911 to 1956, the ubiquitous Jones disarmed his subjects with an unassuming manner. What he took away on film was beyond candid—it was a real moment in time.

While Leslie Jones was working professionally, Jules Aarons was just starting out as a serious amateur. In 1946, while pursuing a master's degree in physics from Boston University, the New York–born Aarons became fascinated by the old neighborhoods of Boston. His "photography of the streets" was captured using a twin-lens Rolleiflex, a camera he calls "sneaky" because it was held at waist level, allowing him to produce a photo without the subject being aware of the camera. Along with the surreptitious nature of the camera came his desire to document "day-to-day life experiences of the people who lived in the city." The result is a stunning array of images, richly portraying the lives of the new immigrants to the West, North, and South End neighborhoods. Almost fifty years later, these photographs remain dynamic. There is an ethereal, familiar quality to them. Looking at the faces, you travel back to the neighborhoods and the life that went on in them.

This book brings together some of the photos by Jones and Aarons used in the television series, plus many others. The majority of the

Leslie Jones photo of the Fish Pier, c. 1935, when the harbor was teeming with fish.

West End street scene, c. 1950.

JULES AARONS

Starting line of the Boston Marathon, Hopkinton, 1948. One hundred forty-three runners, many wearing leather shoes, started the 26.2-mile trek to Boston—a far cry from the One Hundredth Marathon I just completed with 40,000 others.

Nightclubbing, 1945. The Latin Quarter waiter issues his "last call" as the midnight wartime curfew nears.

photographs in Chapters 1 through 5 are from their work; the remaining chapters draw on various private collections. Taken together, I believe these images tell part of the story of Boston fifty years ago. The quotations used throughout the book are from the many interviews I conducted while producing the TV series. Hearing people describe their experiences of this era brought these photographs and much of my research to life for me. I hope you will agree that at least a slice of life as it was lived in Boston from 1930 to 1950 is served up in these 132 pages, and that you will close this book feeling like you "remembered when" or "wondered how."

My gratitude goes out to David Bernstein of WGBH for taking the risk to publish the book; Nancy Lattanzio, my editor, who somehow organized the book to completion in under four months; Mary Cahill Farella for her assistance in countless details; Scott-Martin Kosofsky, whose superb design gave the book life and shape; copyeditor Susan M. Brown, and proofreader Kathryn Blatt; Aaron Schmidt and Mary Beth Dunhouse of the Boston Public Library; Pat Maurer of the Bostonian Society; Lorna Condon of the Society for the Preservation of New England Antiquities; Dick Johnson and Brian Codagnone of the Sports Museum of New England; John Cronin of the *Boston Herald*; the Boston Housing Authority; and many private collectors, such as Ray Barron, Peter McCauley, Bob Pollock, Bob Bachelder, George Altison, Randy Langenbach, Arthur Griffin, Thelma Marcus, Sonny Jones, and Rudy Franchi.

But clearly without the efforts of Leslie Jones and Jules Aarons, this book would not have been possible. My deepest thanks for their significant contribution.

Also a note of thanks to Thomas O'Connor, the narrator of the "Boston: The Way It Was" series and the author of many books on Boston history. With accessible language and style, Professor O'Connor brought the people of the era together with the places and made me want to care about them as I researched their photographs. He has also been very patient with my last-minute queries.

My final thanks go to my son, Max, for his patience and support while I spent many hours at the computer and not with him. I dedicate this book to him. The Boston he is growing up in is very different from the Boston of fifty years ago, but it is still a town that treasures and learns from its past. I think that bodes well for its future.

The City

Circa 1930–1950

"The Custom House Tower was the tallest building in town."

—Rosie Le Cours
50-year veteran Boston cabbie

The Custom House Tower, 1929, taken from the North Station roof. The Elevated railway ran from North Station to South Station along Atlantic Ave. and Commercial St.

Onboard the El, c. 1950. "When you went into Boston, you got all dressed up. I'd put on my best clothes, gloves, and a hat." —former Dorchester resident Lila Rosenbaum

FIFTY YEARS AGO, the views of Boston from the Custom House Tower were commanding, sweeping along the wharves of the waterfront to the winding streets of Scollay Square and Beacon Hill. Lying in the tower's shadow ran the tracks of the Elevated, providing a way in and out of the city. For decades the Custom House Tower, an example of Greek Revival architecture built by Peabody & Stearns, was the tallest building in Boston. Not interested in building skyscrapers like the Empire State Building, city leaders waited until 1928 to modify zoning codes to allow construction of taller buildings.

A civilized skyline is what Bostonians wanted, for a civilized town. The advertising executive Frank Hatch describes Boston during this era as "a rabbit's warren, with meandering streets and alleyways." It was a labyrinth of neighborhood squares and wooden triple-deckers, of brownstone and brick walk-ups.

For a nickel, a subway ride guaranteed an adventure to Downtown Crossing. A trip to Gilchrist's, R. H. White's, or Filene's was like a visit to an old friend. At Christmas the decorated windows of Jordan Marsh were as much a part of the holiday as church. An anniversary or birthday might mean dinner at a fancy downtown hotel. And, of course, Saturdays meant crowding into one of the many Art Deco movie houses along Washington Street. Entering with your friends, you sat two to a seat, ate the box lunch your mother packed, and stayed all day. For a dime.

But watching *The Perils of Pauline* was more than entertainment; it was a welcome relief from reality. In January 1930, a man fell dead of hunger in downtown Boston, the first of many victims of the Depression. Unemployment was 29 percent in the city. For the next ten years, the Depression would worsen the already shaky Boston economy. Banks would fail, countless stores would close, factories and railroad cars would stand empty, even the boisterous Fish Pier would fall quiet as dockworkers lost their jobs.

The forties were meant to be a new era, a recovery from the Depression, but the prosperity was short-lived. With the onslaught of World War II, shortages and rationing made life in Boston, as in other cities, all the more beleaguered. Dish giveaways were used to get people back into the movie houses; dance marathons to the strains of "Moonlight Serenade" raised money for the war effort. Meanwhile, Boston was crumbling, with congested streets and run-down housing.

By 1945 the city was showing the strain. In an editorial that year, the *Globe* called Boston "a hopeless backwater, a tumbled down has-been among cities." Even along elegant Commonwealth Avenue, many of the brownstones were boarded up. Boston had become the dowager aunt, eccentric and shabby, frayed along the edges.

The rogue Irish mayor James Michael Curley, who held some form of elected office from 1914 to 1949, had done little to bring the city back to promised prosperity. Thumbing his nose at the Yankee establishment, Curley called them the "State Street wrecking crew," who descended from "rumrunners and slave traders." As the gap between Yankee Protestant and Irish Catholic grew, the neighborhoods were where the war was waged. While downtown represented the establishment, the ethnic neighborhoods represented Curley's power base. As a result, he used the funds he did receive to build bathhouses and libraries where his constituency lived and to expand the subways and City Hospital. Meanwhile, downtown stood neglected, and even the lights of Scollay Square seemed dim after World War II.

Many war veterans returning home wanted more than run-down Boston could offer. Taking advantage of the G.I. Bill, many soldiers made use of home mortgages and night school. And so began the flight to the suburbs and the era of rooming houses in Boston.

JULES AARONS

Hat sale, Filene's. Hats and gloves were a part of every woman's wardrobe.

North Station, c.1950. Overcoats and fedoras were the fashion statement for men.

JULES AARONS

Faneuil Hall Marketplace, c. 1930, not so different from what it looks like today. The market has been offering up its wares and negotiable prices since colonial times.

"For a dollar, you could get enough fruits and vegetables to last a week."
—Francena Roberson
a South End resident, on shopping during the Depression at Haymarket, Faneuil Hall

". . . and don't slip in any bruised ones."
—A North End resident
keeping a watchful eye on what goes into the bag

Seldom seen view of Haymarket Square showing North Station and the Boston Garden in the background, c. 1948, before construction of the Central Artery and the Callahan Tunnel.

Taking a break from the Dever campaign, c. 1948. A Democrat, Paul Dever succeeded Robert Bradford as governor and served just one term. During his four years in office, he received millions in state funds to improve roads and highways and created the Massachusetts Turnpike Authority in 1952.

JULES AARONS

The City, circa 1930–1950 7

Clearing snow, Tremont St., c. 1933. During one Depression-era snowstorm, over 1,300 men applied to shovel snow for five dollars a day. Mayor Curley hired 1,000 of them, 300 more than were needed.

Washington Street, "Theater Row," 1940. This street was filled with movie houses showing first-run pictures, newsreels, sometimes even stage shows. The cost? Just a dime.

The Boston El taking the turn on Causeway St., c. 1940s. Most of these buildings were demolished during the removal of the West End neighborhood in the early 1960s. The Elevated tracks, however, remain in the same location.

April 19, 1935, Johnny Kelley winning the Boston Marathon. He won another in 1945 and qualified for three Olympic teams between 1936 and 1948. The oldest of ten children, Kelley began his love affair with running at age twelve, when his father took him to Commonwealth Ave. to watch the marathoners pass by.

This page: Onboard the "Penny Ferry," c. 1945. This was one of many ferries in Boston at the time; it departed Eastern Ave. near the Pilot House and crossed the harbor to East Boston. For a nickel, cars were allowed to board.

Facing page: Bean Supper on the Boston Common to benefit the building of the Freedom Trail, 1950. Dating back to colonial Boston, the Common has been the setting for more public life than any other site in the city. The Freedom Trail would help tourists visit Boston's historic sites, or what Mayor John B. Hynes called the charms of "old Dame Boston."

JULES AARONS

The City, circa 1930–1950 13

Facing page: Master marble shooters at the Boys' Marbles Championships, May 1947. Games of marbles were the rage among youngsters on neighborhood playgrounds, culminating in a city-sponsored championship on the Common.

This page: Washington St., c. 1940. Postwar Boston was a tired, run-down city, with elderly and transient residents left in the deteriorating neighborhoods of the inner city. Although the number of Blacks would double during World War II, they still made up less than 10 percent of the city's population by 1950 and lived mostly in the South and West Ends.

JULES AARONS

The South Boston native Cardinal Richard J. Cushing, "the most human of Boston priests," c. 1940. His ability to close the gap between Irish Catholic and Yankee WASP was instrumental in creating the spirit of reform that would sweep Boston in the post-Curley years. Crusty and curmudgeonly, Cushing loved publicity and during religious festivals walked the streets in full ecclesiastical splendor.

The Old Neighborhood

"You'd see the iceman coming down the street and you'd yell, 'Give me a five-cent piece.'"

—Gladys Shapiro
former West Ender

West End soda fountain, c. 1945. Throughout the neighborhood, small businesses catered to local residents and provided places to socialize with friends.

Card players at the Prado, the North End, 1950, beneath the great words of the Founding Fathers.

Previous page: The iceman, West End, late 1940s. Photograph by Jules Aarons.

"YOU WEREN'T AFRAID. There was no fear; people kept their doors open." That's how South End resident Helen Hellman describes life in her neighborhood fifty years ago.

Although many of the ethnic neighborhoods of Boston—the North, South, and West Ends—were depressed economically during the thirties and forties, there was a quality of life in them that far exceeded the annual income of residents. These working-class communities were home to a panoply of ethnic groups. Irish, Italians, Blacks, Hispanics, Asians, Jews, and Poles all lived and worked side by side. "As a kid, you could swear in several different languages," recalls South Ender Jeanette Hajjar. Sonny Jones, a Black West Ender, remembers, "Everybody got along, everybody worked hard."

The Irish immigration to these neighborhoods, which began with the terrible potato famine of the 1840s, was followed by a flood of European immigrants by the turn of the century. As many of these new citizens settled into Boston's historic urban neighborhoods, storefronts, restaurants, and churches reflected the new American melting pot. Small businesses lined congested streets, air in the alleys was rich with the smells of ethnic foods, and laundry lines crisscrossed out windows. During the war, electrical cords were strung from apartment to apartment, creating a lifeline of light even when an unpaid bill caused a shutoff.

By 1930 the diversity of the neighborhoods was solidified, laying the groundwork for the end of the era of Yankee political dominance. But the challenge came not only in City Hall, where Mayor Curley held court, but in the neighborhoods, where political clubs and community organizing had taken hold. In the South End, Dr. Silas Taylor, a Black pharmacist who went by the nickname Shag, got things done by being Curley's Ward 9 boss. Like scores of other ward bosses throughout the city, he worked with the Curley machine to provide jobs and housing for his constituency. South End resident Myra McAdoo remembers Taylor as effective and respected. "He knew everyone in the neighborhood and what they may need. People trusted him for help."

Many Blacks had come to New England to work in shoe factories or shipyards, and they continued to find work here during the war years. By 1950 the Black population had almost doubled in Boston, with many Blacks making their homes in the South End or Roxbury.

But while the grassroots power of a local ward boss guaranteed employment and new libraries in the old neighborhood, it didn't bring new housing. In a strategy known as redlining, banks refused to give home improvement loans or mortgages in areas deemed poor financial risks. The most egregious example of redlining was under way in the West End, the neighborhood between the North End and Scollay Square. As early as 1907, redeveloping this low-income community had been discussed by various civic leaders—the West End's fifty-two acres, in close proximity to downtown, were prime real estate. When the wrecking ball finally did "renew" the neighborhood, the biggest losers were the over 7,000 mostly poor and elderly displaced residents. "My whole family was told to go," recalls Sonny Jones," and as far as I can remember, nobody ever got any money."

The high-priced apartment complex that replaced the West End became a symbol for "urban removal," a public policy gone haywire in the name of progress. What it took away was more than mortar and brick. Many residents still talk about Boston losing its soul when the West End was torn down.

And Sonny Jones, like many residents of the old neighborhood who stayed in Boston, is still waiting for the replacement apartment that was promised him thirty years ago, when the bulldozers came down Spring Street.

A West End girl in front of a kosher meat market, c. 1950.

North End street, c. 1950. "You knew everybody in the neighborhood and they knew you." —South End resident Myra McAdoo.

West End, c. 1940. This corner no longer exists, having been part of the "urban removal" of the West End neighborhood. St. Joseph's is still an active Catholic church, but now it is hidden among high-rise apartments and hospital buildings.

West End laundry day, c. 1945. After World War II, the West End was considered a slum, in line for "urban renewal." But to thousands of elderly immigrants who had fled from repression in Europe, it was home.

JULES AARONS

This page: West End, c. 1940s. Jews began arriving in Boston in large numbers during the 1880s and 1890s, escaping the pogroms in Russia and Poland. By 1910 the Jewish population was over 80,000, with seven Yiddish newspapers and a Yiddish theater. Many Jewish families and businesses were set up in the West End, living and working side by side with Blacks, Italians and Bohemians, Scottish and Irish.

Facing page: North End barbershop, c. 1950. During this era, unions were not only popular but practically mandatory, motivating customers to look in a business's window for the union sign, guaranteeing good workmanship and a fair wage.

JULES AARONS

JULES AARONS

North End drugstore, c. 1950. By this time, the North End was all Italian, with the Irish and Eastern European immigrants having long since left the neighborhood for South Boston and Dorchester.

North End, Perry's Pool Room, c. 1945.

"It didn't take much, and we didn't have much in those days."
—Dorothea James
Revere resident

North End hot dog stand, corner of Hanover and Blackstone streets, 1937.

Old reliable grinder, Back Bay, c. 1930s. Like the iceman, the knife and scissors sharpener would make his way through the streets of the city, usually followed by a group of children watching him work.

Tyler St., Chinatown, 1941. Not until 1890 did Boston have a permanent Chinese community, in the South Cove neighborhood. Many Chinese came from the West Coast, where they had labored in the gold mines or on the tracks of the transcontinental railroad.

The first commencement of the Quong Kow Chinese School, 1931. Quong Kow was a mission school designed to help first-generation Chinese immigrants learn English and get an education.

A CYO (Catholic Youth Organization) boys' baseball team lights a candle before the big game, c. 1950, Mission Church, Mission Hill neighborhood. After Archbishop William Henry O'Connell became a cardinal, he began a series of changes to separate the Catholic church from the Protestant denominations. The CYO, organized in Boston in 1911, was his way of encouraging Catholic youth to socialize together instead of with non-Catholics at neighborhood Y's or in secular scout troops.

Cathedral of the Holy Cross, as seen through the Washington St. Elevated tracks, c. 1940. This church created the dividing line between the Catholics in the South End and the Protestants in the Back Bay.

American Legion parade down Columbus Ave., 1930. The Savoy Cafe, Hotel Kimball, and Braddock Drug were all South End landmarks.

Breadline, c. 1931, 42 Hanover St., North End. In the years leading up to World War II, soup kitchens and breadlines served the many men out of work. Pawnshops around Scollay Square and the neighborhoods filled with jewelry as jobs were lost and families cashed in their belongings for food and utility money.

North End neighborhood beach, c. 1927. During this era, the beaches along Atlantic Ave. were clean enough to swim in.

"When I think back, it was peaceful. Children used to run through the alleys and climb fences."

—Helen Johnson
longtime South Ender

North End, 1950.

JULES AARONS

North End windows, c. 1950.

"You'd walk down the street on a summer evening and you wouldn't miss a word of Walter Winchell."

—Jeanette Hajjar
South End resident

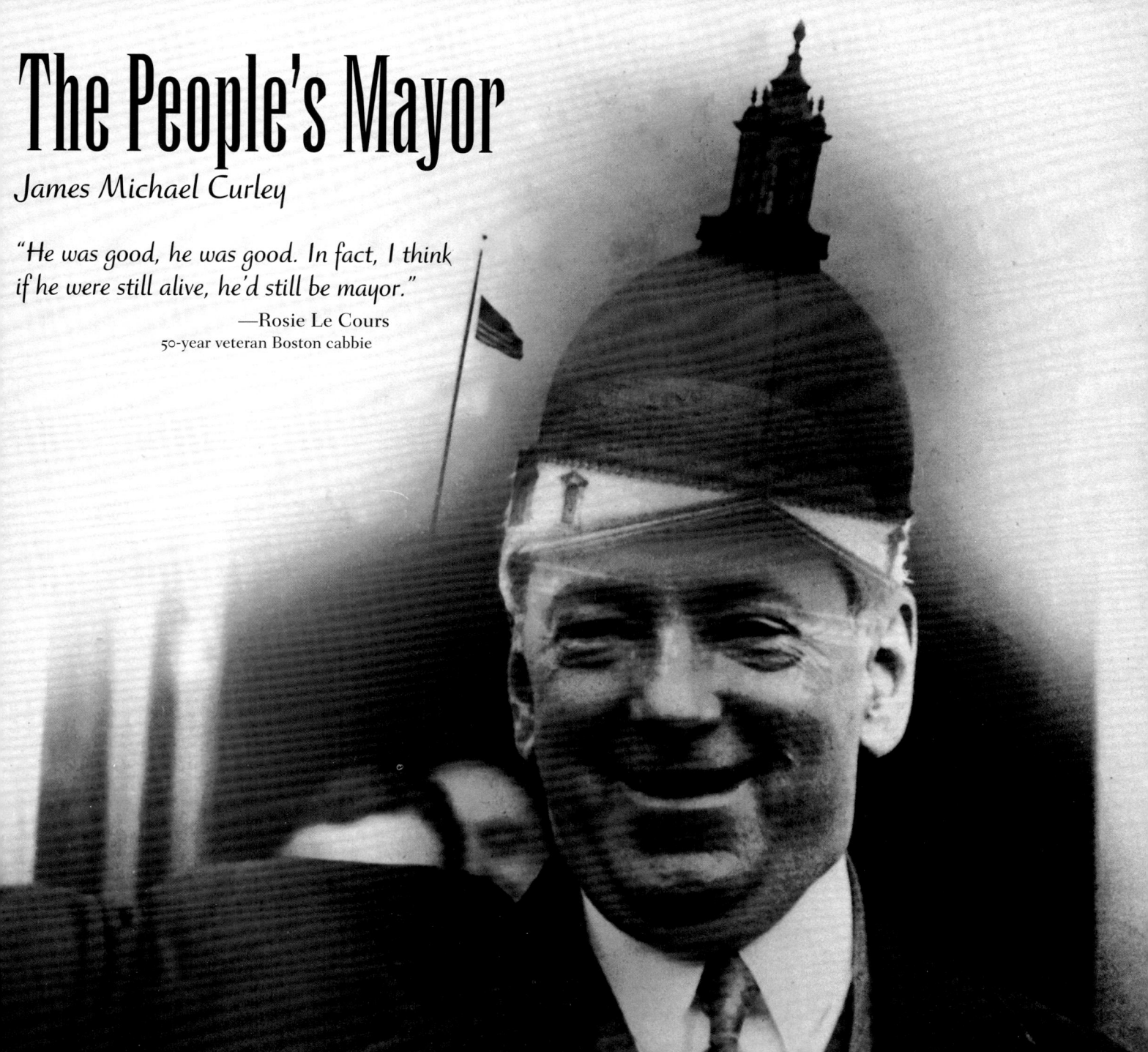

The People's Mayor

James Michael Curley

"He was good, he was good. In fact, I think if he were still alive, he'd still be mayor."

—Rosie Le Cours
50-year veteran Boston cabbie

The Curley sound wagon, 1949, with the mayor aboard campaigning for his fifth term against John B. Hynes.

Yankee Republican Henry Cabot Lodge, reelected senator in November 1946. Ten years earlier, he had beaten Curley in his first run for the seat.

Previous page: James Michael Curley, c.1935.

I

T'S HARD TO IMAGINE James Michael Curley holding any political office today, let alone serving four terms as mayor (one while in prison for mail fraud), two terms in congress, and one term as governor. But from 1910, when he was first elected to Congress, until after World War II, when he served his last term as mayor, Curley didn't just dominate the political scene in Boston, he defined it.

Curley was born of modest means on Northampton Street, in Roxbury's Ward 17, on November 20, 1874. With no formal education beyond grammar school, Curley was self-taught; he read voraciously and early on developed a taste for the finer things in life. Determined to reinvent himself, he even developed a variation in his Boston accent, creating the "Oxford undertaker" persona. During one of his early campaigns, the *Boston Evening Transcript* described him as "born, not with a silver spoon, but with a wooden ladder in his mouth, which he proceeded forthwith to climb."

Climb he did, over, under, and around anything possible to get elected. His first election for mayor came when John "Honey Fitz" Fitzgerald dropped out of the race citing ill health. But many say the real reason was Curley's threat to expose Fitzgerald's alleged tryst with a cigarette girl named Toodles! Refusing support from the Democratic committee, whom he called "a collection of chowderheads," and reviling the Republican, Yankee establishment—he claimed that "the Anglo Saxon is a joke, a new and better America is here"—Curley went directly to the neighborhoods for support. "His people," the ethnic dockworkers, store clerks, and housekeepers, would never let him down. They knew Jim Curley had humble roots and, more important, never forgot them.

Curley relished the feeling of power when he helped someone out, believing a job to be more honorable than "the dole." When the Republicans refused any state funding for downtown Boston, calling his administration corrupt, Curley rebuilt the neighborhoods instead. Through his chain of ward bosses, the Curley machine built new roads, parks, and subway lines. With his inimitable charisma and charm, Curley directed his rhetoric around the emerging class and social divisions. But as the gap between Irish Catholic and Yankee Protestant widened, so did the gap between downtown and the neighborhoods.

Not caring if the city, which represented the despised Yankee establishment, was run-down, Curley stood by as Boston got more decrepit by the year. But despite (or maybe because of) his reputation on Beacon Hill, he was revered in the neighborhoods. A poll taken after his second felony conviction found that 60 percent of Bostonians thought he was still doing a good job as mayor. In 1947, after he'd exhausted all his appeal efforts, over 100,000 Bostonians signed a petition asking President Truman to grant Curley "executive clemency" from his mail fraud conviction. Although Truman refused to go that far, a presidential pardon did shorten Curley's prison sentence, and he was released from the state penitentiary in Danbury, Connecticut, after serving five months.

By 1950, however, approaching his eighth decade and in failing health, Curley would reluctantly concede his days were over. Returning veterans wanted to live in a city with a vision for the future, not one divided and polarized by different interests. Change came in the candidacy of John B. Hynes. A quiet man and a career bureaucrat, the antithesis of the "people's mayor," Hynes would defeat Curley three times and serve ten years as mayor over the next decade.

Curley's antics—from the extra telephone on his desk that was said to be a direct line to his bookie to his regular appearances at the Old Howard burlesque house—were all part of this uniquely Boston character. He was an original if there ever was one; it's hard to imagine Boston without Curley during this era, although many may have wished for just that fifty years ago.

April 15, 1942, "Lefty" Leverett Saltonstall, who had defeated Curley in the governor's race four years earlier, throws out the first ball at the Red Sox opener.

House at 311 Chelsea St., East Boston, October 1929. Curley would go on to win this race and a record fourth term in City Hall. During this era, he was elected so often that the Republican-controlled legislature finally passed a law making it impossible for Curley to succeed himself.

Curley, 1945, greeting Archbishop Cushing, who at the time was emerging as spiritual leader of Boston's Catholic population. Both men were masterful in their public relations efforts, but while Curley taunted the WASP establishment, Cushing reached out to non-Catholics, attempting to close the gap that had emerged between groups.

"He was a prominent looking person, full face, he was a guy who would steal from one and give to another."

—Rosie Le Cours

The "People's Mayor," as he loved to be called, greeting "Thor" in his last campaign for mayor.

Facing page: Governor Curley wearing a Sioux warbonnet, with Princess Big Elk of the Oglala Indian tribe and his daughter Mary Curley, 1935.

This page: James Michael Curley, in his chinoiserie, with Gertrude Dennis Curley, c. 1940. After Curley's wife Mary died of cancer at age forty-five, he married Gertrude, a widow.

President Roosevelt on the arm of Mayor Curley, 1934. Although Curley said in his campaigns that he had close ties to FDR and that Boston would benefit financially from the connection, in the end his "work and wages" promise would receive little federal funding to back it up.

Three generations of the Boston Irish political forces—Mayor Curley, Governor Maurice Tobin, and congressional candidate John F. Kennedy—at a VFW convention, 1946. Grandson of two Democratic ward bosses, the young war hero signified a new era of politics in Boston. Even his dress reflected something different: seen here in subdued Navy dress blues, JFK refused to wear the typical wide-brimmed fedora, and his suits were classic and refined, not splashy like those of most "pols" of the era.

"*He was an enormously entertaining figure, a great actor.*"

—John Kenneth Galbraith
economist and Harvard professor

Curley and the *Mona Lisa*, c. 1945.

Boston Goes to War

"There was a rush to enlist. The Navy would take you at seventeen, if you didn't want to wait for the Army at eighteen."

—Veteran Ray Barron
noted Boston bandleader

Pvt. Joseph Barisano—Ray Barron—Fallow-field, England, April 1944.

Defense bonds ad, c. 1943. During the war, the advertising industry founded the War Advertising Council, a nonprofit service agency designed to use advertising to strengthen the war effort.

Previous page: Castle Island, c. 1943. After U-boats were sighted off the coast of New Jersey, guards kept watch on Boston Harbor.

ONLY TWENTY YEARS after World War I was over, Bostonians were facing another war. And the generation dancing to the strains of Glenn Miller at the Totem Pole would be inexorably changed by fighting it.

The effort to embrace the war did not happen overnight, however. The city was socially and politically divided, with the Yankees claiming a moral obligation to defend England's fight for civilization, while the Irish Catholic sentiment was summed up in the popular phrase of the day "Let them keep it over there."

The deep distrust of President Roosevelt in the ethnic neighborhoods came from the attitude that "Rosenfeld," as he was called by some, was too friendly toward the British and the Jews. Irish Catholics who listened to the anti-Semitic radio broadcasts of Father Coughlin remembered FDR's speech at the Boston Garden, when he promised "Your boys are not going to be sent into any foreign wars." Even the stories about Nazi death camps fell on skeptical ears. Having heard of heinous crimes in Belgium during World War I only to learn later that they were part of a government propaganda effort, people were harder to convince.

Until Pearl Harbor was bombed by the Japanese on December 7, 1941.

Now the city united in support of defeating the Germans and the Japanese. The mood changed overnight as young men enlisted, eager to become part of history. On Monday, December 8, over a thousand enthusiasts signed up at the Boston Post Office recruiting center. Thousands more followed them before the week was over. "We knew we'd get drafted, but if you joined up, they guaranteed you could finish the year of college you were in," remembers Boston College Professor of History Tom O'Connor, who was in his freshman year at BC in 1943. "This was an army of teenagers who left and would be faced with making life and death decisions during the war."

But it was not just the young men of Boston supporting the war. "This was everybody's war," says O'Connor. Through a carefully designed poster campaign, women and children were told what was expected of them, from buying war bonds to recycling pots and pans. Victory Gardens grew vegetables so grocery chains could send food to troops instead of selling it retail, children saved scraps of wood for heating, and nylon ended up as parachutes instead of as stockings on women's legs.

"Save" was more than a buzzword—it became a way of life. Conserving and doing without became the rule. From gasoline to shoes, it was your duty to make things last. And some things, like meat, you learned to live without. Meatless Tuesdays and Porkless Wednesdays meant beans without the franks, potatoes without the pot roast. The *Globe* and *Herald Traveler* food sections were filled with recipes using everything but meat.

While all those who were stateside were expected to do their part, there were also things you didn't do. "It was the old 'slip of the lip sinks the ship,'" recalls O'Connor. "And a certain paranoia engaged you in the effort. For instance, if you received a letter from your husband and he told you where he was stationed, you never revealed the location to anyone. Nazi agents could be listening on the corner, wherever," he explains. But some of this paranoia was warranted. On the West Coast the Japanese flew surveillance balloons, while German U-boats were sighted off the coast of New Jersey.

Even schoolchildren got into the act by learning how to spot Nazi airplanes. After all, according to O'Connor's high school cadet training colonel, "It was only a matter of time before the war was going to be fought here."

Blackout advertisement, c. 1943. Fearing enemy attack, Americans took "dimout time" very seriously.

Red Sox slugger Ted Williams takes the Navy oath, 1942.

South Station Elevated tracks, 1942. Throughout the city, crews took down the steel girders of the El, which were recycled for the war effort.

Tremont St., 1943. This captured submarine was displayed to encourage the purchase of war bonds.

"In 1943, Americans were told to use it up, wear it out, make it do, or do without."

—Ray Barron

Wartime meat shortage, 1943.

Training for factory work, 1943. As the men headed off to war, "Rosie the Riveter" headed for work. Whether it was welding in a Quincy factory or assembling car parts in South Boston, women left the kitchen for work during World War II.

War Days, c. 1944. Looking for U-boats in Boston Harbor, spotting Nazi airplanes, or making sure your gas mask worked made the war very real. "It was only a matter of time," remarked one military training officer.

U.S. Coast Guard recruits, 1943. After the bombing of Pearl Harbor, thousands of young men enlisted, departing from South Station to parts unknown. For most this was their first trip outside the city.

"Everybody working but Dad," 1944. Through a well-orchestrated poster campaign, children were encouraged to get involved in the war effort. Working in the family Victory Garden and collecting wood to use as fuel were ways of doing your part.

Radcliffe College, 1943. Although most women would quit working and return home after the war, the seeds had been sown for the battle for equality.

"The war was over, everyone was so grateful that their boyfriend, husband, or brother came home safe. You were satisfied with a lot less."

—Lila Rosenbaum
former Dorchester resident

This page: VJ Day, 1945, downtown Boston. Sailors and girlfriends celebrate Japan's surrender.

Facing page: Besides the emotional scars of war, many veterans ended up physically maimed, facing a difficult adjustment upon their return stateside.

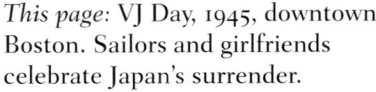

Boston Traveler headline, May 7, 1945. Carrier Fred Apt sells the biggest news of the war on Tremont St.

Scollay Square

and the Old Howard

*"Scollay Square was the closest
thing to a four-letter word
you could have."*

—Bob Bachelder
last bandleader at the
Totem Pole Ballroom

The Old Howard, c. 1900. Once an Adventist Tabernacle Church, the Old Howard attracted a different type of congregation when the burlesque queens took to the stage.

Previous page: Scollay's Olympia Theatre, c. 1930. This landmark, built in 1912, had movies running from 9:00 A.M. to 11:00 P.M. The Olympia charged ten cents for a movie and a nickel for a bag of candy.

NESTLED BETWEEN Faneuil Hall, the North End, and the West End, Scollay Square was the destination of choice for sailors who docked at Commonwealth Pier during World War II. But it wasn't just sailors taking in the sights. Scollay Square was once the heart and soul of Boston. Simply put, everyone went there.

In its earliest days, the square was home to eccentrics and geniuses. Thomas Edison invented the automatic vote counter in a storefront off Brattle Square. Famed architect Charles Bulfinch developed many buildings in historic downtown Boston with William Scollay, son of the real estate mogul for whom the square was named. Various colonial governors made their homes in Scollay Square, along streets with names like Elm, Howard, and Pemberton. Close to the waterfront and bustling trade business of the wharves, the square would eventually become home to America's first streetcar line, whose tracks would end in front of the Scollay Building.

But it was burly, burlesque, that a visit to Scollay Square was really all about, and the home of burlesque was the Old Howard. The Old Howard was America's oldest theater, built originally as a church. By 1900 vaudeville had taken over, and showgirls pranced at the Old Howard. As the centerpiece act of vaudeville, the striptease, complete with stage orchestra and chorus line, was all about the illusion of sex and nudity. It not only appealed to the bald-headed old men who "only went for the comics" but attracted some of Boston's great thinkers as well. After one vaudeville show, Justice Oliver Wendell Holmes remarked, "Thank God I am a man of low taste." The theater was even nicknamed the Old Harvard because of the number of Harvard undergraduates who warmed its seats. Headline stripper Ann Corio remembers one student in particular: "JFK was in love with a stripper by the name of Peaches Strange. He was a regular at the Old Howard."

In the 1930s, at Corio's suggestion, midnight shows for unescorted ladies only were added to the lineup. As a result, the Old Howard finally installed a ladies' room. But members of the Watch and Ward Society, many of whom were women, were not interested in this accommodation. They called the Old Howard the "shame of Boston" and in 1933 succeeded in having Mayor Curley close it down for thirty days—despite the regularity with which he and Mrs. Curley went to the theater. Going so far as to call it publicly one of Boston's "great institutions," Curley showed once again his political instincts. Placating both the temperance group and the fans of burly, the mayor reopened the Old Howard with the agreement that the city censor would make an occasional unannounced visit. "The ticket taker at the front door would hit a buzzer letting everyone know the censor was coming in," recalls Mike Ionucci, Corio's husband. "Then the strip would become Rebecca of Sunnybrook Farm."

If the Old Howard was full or closed down, there was always the Crawford House, another of the three burlesque houses in the square. Here patrons could see Sally Keith twirl her tassels or Sally Rand swish her fans.

During the war, when tattoo parlors, shooting galleries, hucksters, and bookies lined the streets, Scollay Square was still considered a safe neighborhood—definitely a bit on the wild side but relatively free from crime. Neighbors, tourists, politicians, and of course patrons of the Old Howard would crowd the streets, anxious for a taste of Joe and Nemo's famous hot dogs.

But after the war, with no more sailors docking in Boston's Barbary Coast and little support from city leaders, Scollay Square went into serious decline. With the adjoining West End neighborhood slated for "urban renewal," it was only a matter of time before Scollay Square met a similar fate.

The Crawford House on Brattle St. as it looked during Prohibition, c. 1930. Originally built as a hotel in 1848, it had the first passenger elevator in the country and attracted such dignitaries as Massachusetts senator Daniel Webster.

Left: Scollay Square, c. 1940. Located just beyond Washington St., the square consisted of twenty-two streets lined with tattoo parlors, pawnshops, shooting galleries, and burlesque houses.

Above: Commonwealth Pier, c. 1945. Scollay Square was so popular with the sailors it was said that PT boats out in the Atlantic would radio each other, "How are things in Scollay Square?"

"Scollay Square was everyman's place, and you didn't get slighted for going in there either."

—Francena Roberson
a South End resident

Doorway of the Hotel Imperial, 27 Howard St., c. 1945.

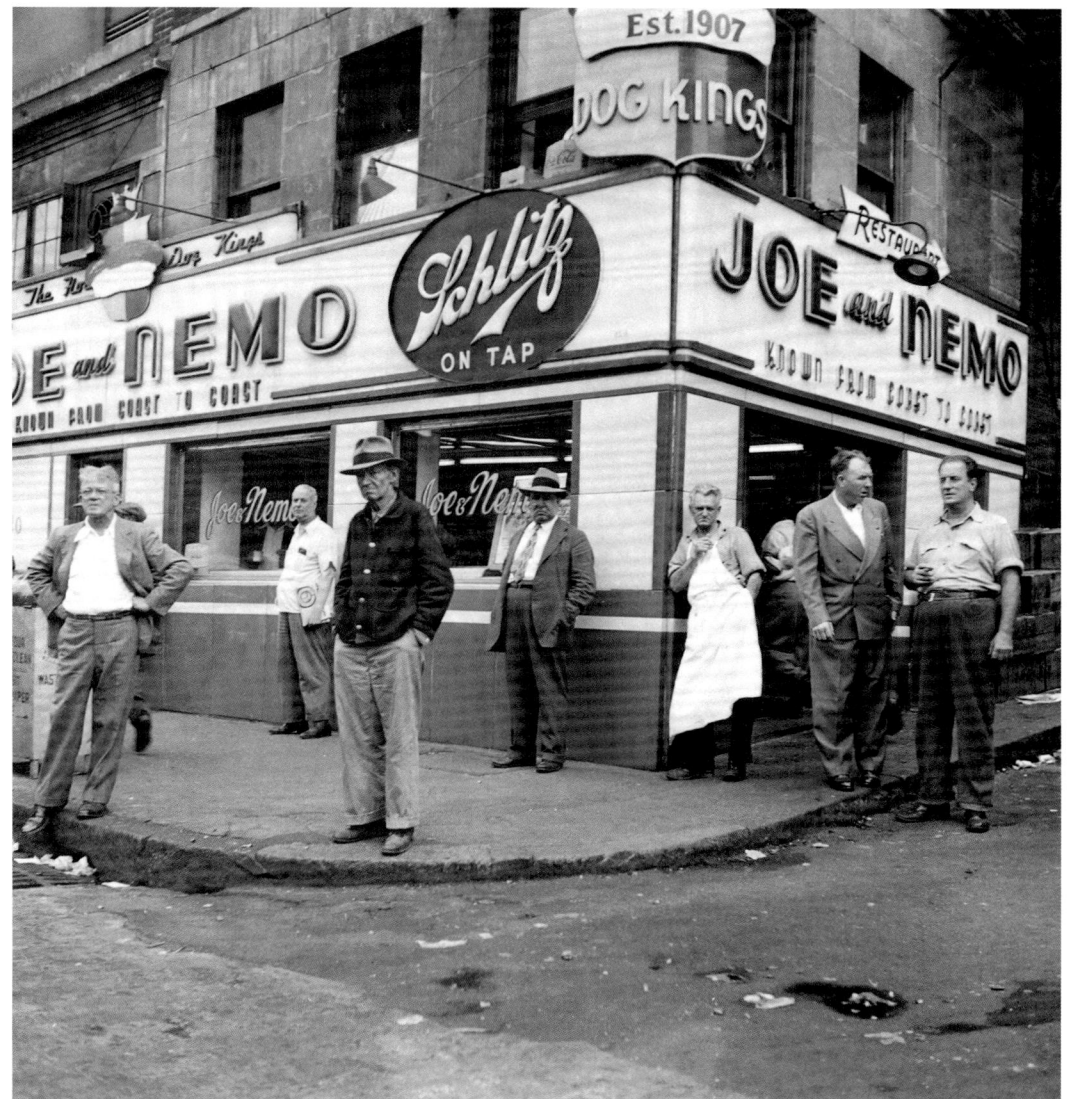

JULES AARONS

"There was a hustle and bustle to the square. People would go up the street to Joe and Nemo's, where, for ten cents, you could get a hot dog and glass of soda."

—Ralph Saya
Old Howard projectionist

Joe and Nemo's, c. 1950. Joe and Nemo's was opened in 1907 by a barber named Joe Merlino and Anthony "little Nemo" Caloggero. The two were not related when they started out, but when they married sisters, it became a "family business."

"Jimmy," a Scollay
Square newspaper
vendor, c. 1950.

Sally Rand, the fan dancer, c. 1940. Known for her creative use of fans during her burlesque act, Rand was a favorite at the Old Howard.

"The doorman was hired especially because he knew all the censors in town, so when one came through the front door, he'd hit a button, a red light would start flashing in the footlights, and people backstage would start yelling, 'Sunday school, Sunday school.'"

—Ralph Saya
Old Howard projectionist

Burlesque poster inside the Old Howard, c. 1950, featuring "the darling of burlesque," Ann Corio.

Ann Corio before her stage show, September 1936. Known for leaving much up to the imagination, the burlesque diva would deliver her infamous line "I can't take that off, I'll catch cold."

Scollay Square, c. 1950. After the war, isolation crept into the square. Over the next decade, the wrecking ball would cut a swath through the square's streets, replacing them with a new government complex.

Opposite: Local favorite "Sonny" William Jones (on drums) and friends jam in a club, c. 1949. According to Jones, "You could not go on a job unless you were dressed up or with a suit and tie on."

Old Howard sign, c. 1961. When a mysterious fire gutted the interior of the Old Howard, it signaled the end of an era for burlesque and Scollay Square.

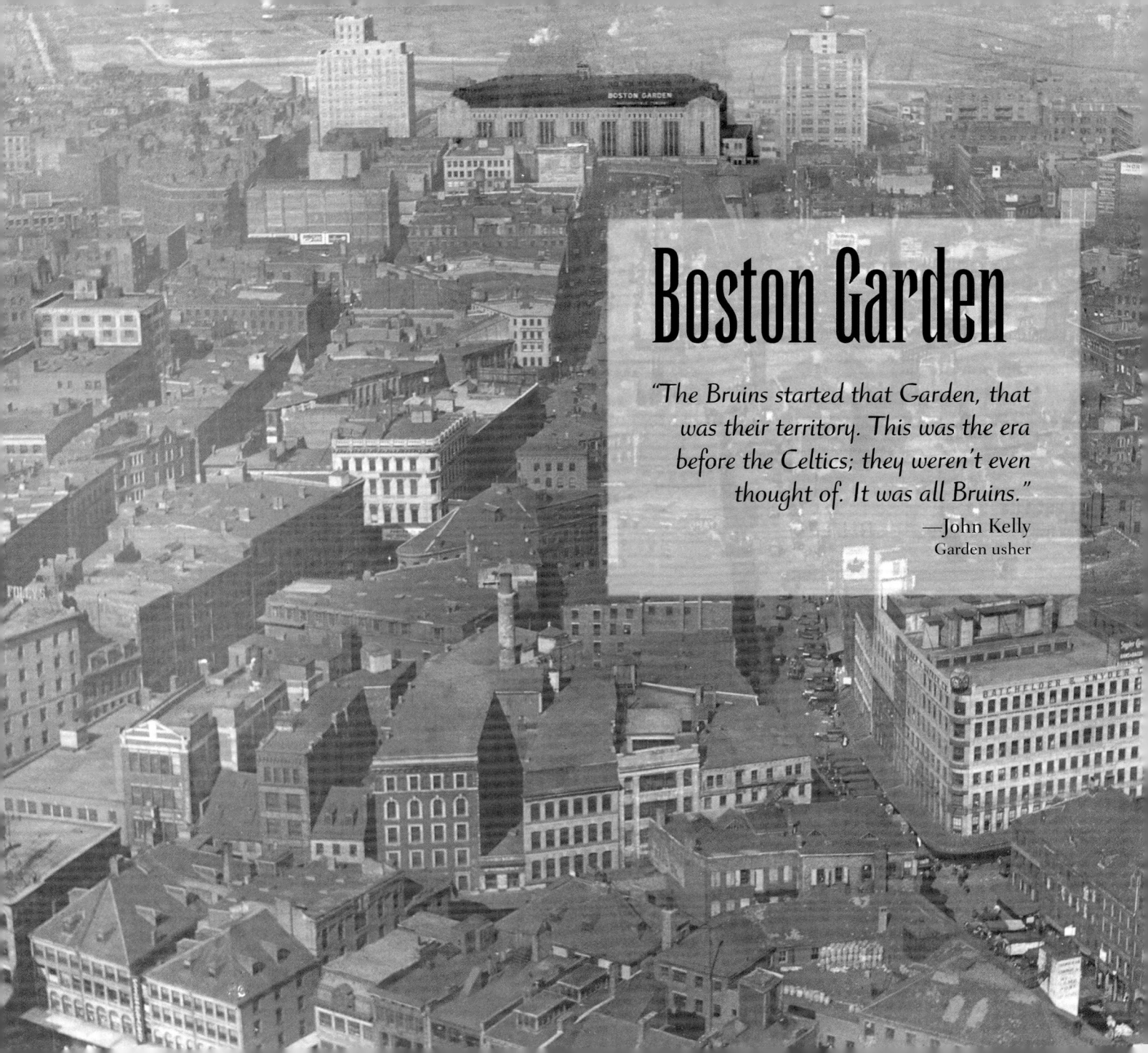

Boston Garden

"The Bruins started that Garden, that was their territory. This was the era before the Celtics; they weren't even thought of. It was all Bruins."

—John Kelly
Garden usher

Dick "Honey Boy" Finnegan of Dorchester, publicity photo, 1928.

Opening night ticket, price, $2.00.

Wᴵᴛʜ ᴛʜᴇ sᴜᴄᴄᴇss of Madison Square Garden under his belt, the entrepreneur Tex Rickard decided in 1928 to add another link to his chain of entertainment empires. For months Causeway Street shook as steel pilings were driven into the ground across from North Station.

On opening night, cars lined the surrounding streets, filled with local and national celebrities waiting to attend the premiere. The warm-up act was an Army private who, blindfolded, assembled a machine gun in forty-seven seconds! Then the crowd went wild over the main event, a boxing match between Dick "Honey Boy" Finnegan of Dorchester and Andre Routis. When the local boy walked away with the featherweight title, the Garden's history had begun.

"The place was built for boxing," remembers another local champion, Tony DeMarco. "You felt like the crowd was right on top of you when you were in the middle of that ring." DeMarco should know. Not a seat or a space in standing room remained as he "fought like a lion" until the knockout in the fourteenth round secured his title as 1955 welterweight champion.

But boxing alone couldn't sustain the crowds and pay off the overhead, especially during the Depression. So the building manager, Walter Brown, figured out other ways to bring in the masses: ice skating shows, golf tournaments, roller derbies, track meets, political and religious rallies, even an indoor ski jump in 1936, along with the usual big-top events like the circus and rodeos.

But in the thirties, the main program at the Garden was the Bruins. And no wonder, with players like Eddie Shore, Woodie Dumart, and Milt Schmidt smacking the puck around. "In the 1938–39 season, we won the Stanley Cup; in 1940–41, we did it again. We played for the same salary every year, and we didn't get a five cent increase," remembers Hall of Famer Schmidt. "That's just the way it was."

The condition of the Garden was also "just the way it was." Parquet floor sweeper Rudy "Spider" Edwards says the building had "rats the size of shoeboxes," steaming floors beneath the parquet (brought on by the ice underneath), and dead zones in the floor. Milt Schmidt remembers another "quaint aspect" of the Garden. "The trains in those days used to come in right underneath and you'd feel the vibration right under you. Then there were the times when the ice was only a quarter of an inch thick in some places and you'd be falling all over the place as the crowd was giving you a hard time, not knowing you were tripping because your skates were hitting the cement floor underneath."

But despite all the Garden's eccentricities, attendance records were broken year after year. The number of people who actually snuck into the Garden, however, became as much a part of its history as the performers. "We knew every way in, from the roof, from the back, from the side doors, we'd sneak in and hang down to the gallery," remembers North End resident Joe Coppola. "They'd even sneak in the heating ducts," according to the fifty-year veteran usher John Kelly. "Security would meet them at the end of the opening and they'd be covered with dirt."

For over six decades, obstructed views and all, the Boston Garden provided sweet memories. It was, in the words of the longtime Bruins fan Marge Prodanis, "like an old friend, just like an old friend. And we had a great time."

Above right: Boston Garden program, c. 1930s. Dusting off the yellow seats by hand.

Right: The welterweight champion of 1955, Tony DeMarco. "The Garden was shaking the night he won his title. From the highest to the lowest, they all adored Tony." —North Ender Joe Coppola

Page 75: Bird's-eye view of the West End, Scollay Square, and the Boston Garden, c. 1930. Taken from the Custom House Tower, this photograph shows the decline the neighborhoods had suffered by the middle of the Depression, making their "urban renewal" inevitable by the late fifties.

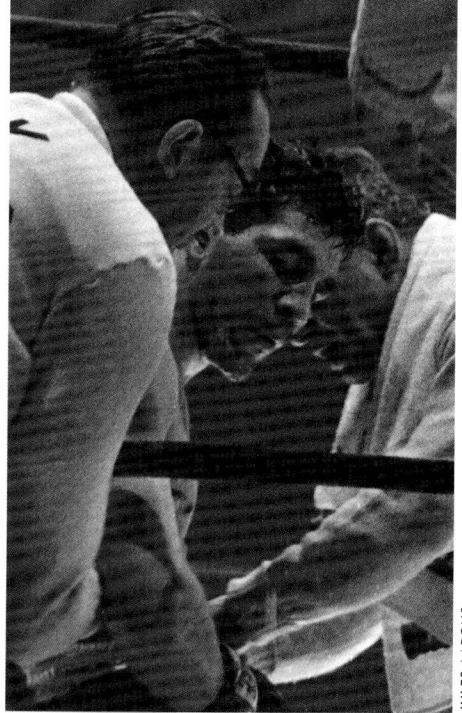

JULES AARONS

Above: Roller Skating Vanities program, Boston Garden, 1944. The building manager, Walter Brown, was known to be a marketing genius and booked acts such as this one to attract more than the boxing or Bruins crowds.

"*Back in those days, the Celtics would be lucky to get a few thousand fans.*"
— John Kelly
Garden usher

Below: Official program, 1946, the year the Celtics began playing at the Garden.

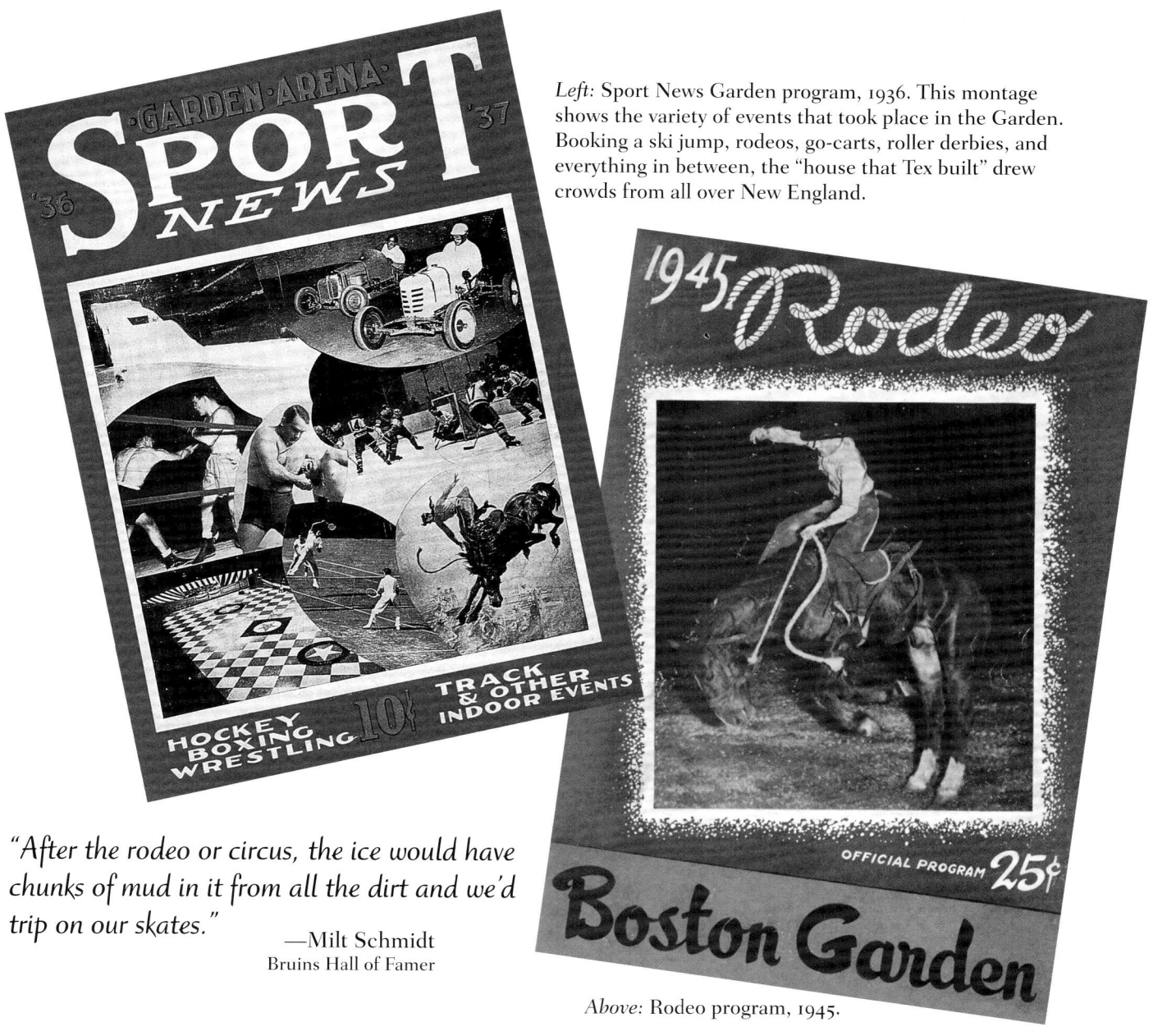

Left: Sport News Garden program, 1936. This montage shows the variety of events that took place in the Garden. Booking a ski jump, rodeos, go-carts, roller derbies, and everything in between, the "house that Tex built" drew crowds from all over New England.

"After the rodeo or circus, the ice would have chunks of mud in it from all the dirt and we'd trip on our skates."
—Milt Schmidt
Bruins Hall of Famer

Above: Rodeo program, 1945.

"Those were the days when agents and lawyers didn't negotiate contracts, players did." —Milt Schmidt

The Bruins locker room, c. 1930.

The Stanley Cup winners in the locker room, 1938–39 season. The future Hall of Famer
Milt Schmidt is Number 15, and "Edmonton Express" Eddie Shore is Number 2.

"There were spots in that floor where the ball would completely lose its bounce, just go dead. And of course that's where the team would try to send it."

—Rudy "Spider" Edwards
parquet floor sweeper

The Celtics in action at the Garden, c. 1950s.

Bruins Hockey clinic on a pond in Newton, with Marty Barry, c. 1930.

A Curley for Governor rally against Leverett Saltonstall, 1938. James Michael Curley's political rallies at the Garden were a mixture of smoke, mirrors, and obstructed views. In this race Curley would lose to the Yankee Republican because of what Saltonstall called "my South Boston face."

Emmett Kelly, the famed Ringling
Brothers, Barnum & Bailey circus
clown, with two-year-old Robert
Hermines, Boston Garden, 1946.

The circus comes to town, 1948, passing
by the Common on Tremont St.

That Big Band Sound

"It was crowded, it was always crowded."
—Thelma Marcus,
about the Cocoanut Grove

Menu for the Cocoanut Grove, 1940. Dinner and dancing could cost as little as $1.50.

The cover to a photo holder for the Latin Quarter, a club in the Bay Village section of Boston, c. 1940.

Previous page: Thelma and Alfred Marcus, outside the Cocoanut Grove, Piedmont St., Boston, 1942

"THERE WERE SO MANY nightclubs, it was so great. For three dollars you had dinner. We used to call it a floor show." That's how the musician and promoter Ray Barron characterizes the club scene in Boston in the forties. As the manager of the Hi-Hat, a dinner and dance club on Mass. Ave. in the South End, Barron remembers when the music played till the wee hours of the morning, with Count Basie, Sabby Lewis, and Stan Getz jamming at Wally's or the Wigwam after finishing their gigs downtown. This was the era of jazz, when musicians like Duke Ellington, Cootie Williams, and Fats Waller headlined the clubs. One South End resident, Tommy Johnson, remembers, "You had bands playing every night. People would be walking up the street having a great time."

In town trolleys would run up and down Columbus Avenue, filled with well-dressed, well-mannered patrons of the clubs. From the South End to Scollay Square, people would travel in groups or as couples, enjoying the safe nightlife of the era.

Clubs like the Latin Quarter or the Cocoanut Grove set the stage for many a birthday or anniversary celebration. During the war, the former West Ender Gladys Shapiro recalls, "A lot of the parties were held at the Cocoanut Grove for the boys going overseas. That was the custom at the time."

November 28, 1942, was supposed to be a night of celebration. But after a 55–12 upset loss to Holy Cross at Fenway Park that cold and blustery fall day, Boston College fans and players stayed home instead of going to the planned Cocoanut Grove victory party. As a result, the team and their fans were not trapped inside the inferno that engulfed the Grove that night.

Everyone in Boston, it seems, knew of someone who died in the Grove fire. Over fifty years later, the deep pain and loss remain. George Graney, a firefighter who was at the club, remembers the night: "There was no fire showing at the one entrance, just heavy black smoke." It was the smoke of plastic decorations that would prove toxic to those inside the overcrowded nightclub.

Treatment at area hospitals with a new drug, called penicillin, would save those who were rescued in time. But 492 others would die in what turned out to be the second worst single-building fire in American history. "With the war coming on, what we learned treating the burns proved to be a valuable asset," comments firefighter Graney.

Meanwhile, in Newton, another trolley ran along Commonwealth Avenue. The stop that was crowded with throngs of young couples was Norumbega, home of the famed Totem Pole Ballroom.

Built in 1930 with an imposing dance floor and massive stage, which was flanked by two gigantic totem poles, the ballroom was known for its intimate lighting and velvet couches. Patrons were guaranteed an inviting, romantic evening. But the Pole had its rules, too, and they were rarely questioned. Attendance was for couples only—no stags, alcohol, or bobby socks allowed, except during the war, when there was a shortage of nylon stockings. And then there was the "no breaking" rule. If you don't know what that is, ask someone older to explain.

The Totem Pole was called the premiere ballroom in New England, but what it represented went beyond the physical structure. Together with "music you could dance to," the Pole and so many of the nightclubs of the era created a milieu for people who were coming of age. This period, defined musically by the strains of Glenn Miller and Count Basie, would make a profound impression on those who grew up during the Depression and World War II. Through it they would come to define their time and place in history.

Top: The entrance sign to Norumbega Park.

Middle: Nickel Day, c. 1940, Norumbega Park.

Bottom: An MDC police boat cuts through the flock of paddleboats on the Charles River at Norumbega, c. 1940.

Above: Ad for the Fourth of July celebration with Emory Daugherty at the Totem Pole, c. 1945.

Advertisement for the Totem Pole Ballroom, c. 1945, "the utmost in refinement." Dancing took place nightly to the sounds of Big Band music; admission was $1.35 per couple, or included with the cost of dinner next door at the Normandie.

"You thought you were in heaven, with the lights, and the deep, soft couches with the high sides around them, you'd sit there and steal a kiss, which we thought was so daring."

—Lila and Albert Rosenbaum
Totem Pole patrons

The original Totem Pole Band, Emory Daugherty and his Tom-Tom Boys, c. 1940, flanked by the famous totem poles. Center stage is a WNAC radio microphone, which brought the show live to those who couldn't be there.

Above, right: Those famous divans, c. 1950.

Left: Hi-Hat Club, Mass. Ave., South End, Boston, as depicted in a postcard, c. 1950. The club was famous for its two-dollar barbecue chicken dinners.

Below: Gathered at the Hi-Hat in 1949 are, left to right: Joe Roland, Howard McGhee, Count Basie, Oscar Pettiford, Ray Barron, Dave Coleman, and Stan Getz.

Above: Ads for the Sabby Lewis Orchestra jam session, which took place at the Hi-Hat on Sundays from 3:00 to 6:00 P.M.

Right: Known for his prowess on the drums, the local drummer William "Baggy" Grant was in demand when the big bands came through Boston, c. 1948.

A night out at the Cocoanut Grove, watching the chorus line on roller skates, 1942.

A bar ticket from the
Cocoanut Grove, c. 1940.

COCOANUT GROVE
50¢
For Bar Use Only
GLOBE TICKET COMPANY, BOSTON
044670

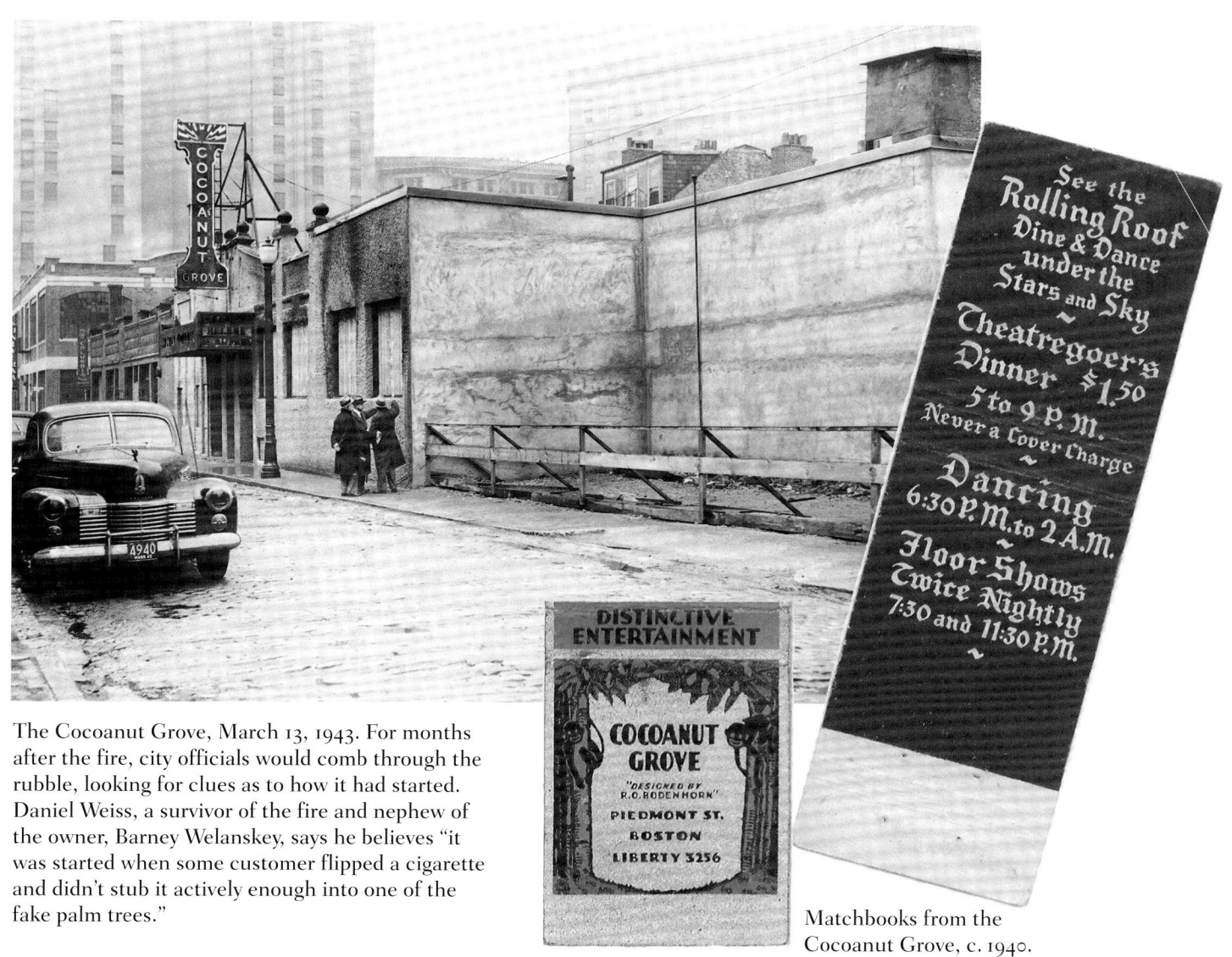

The Cocoanut Grove, March 13, 1943. For months after the fire, city officials would comb through the rubble, looking for clues as to how it had started. Daniel Weiss, a survivor of the fire and nephew of the owner, Barney Welanskey, says he believes "it was started when some customer flipped a cigarette and didn't stub it actively enough into one of the fake palm trees."

DISTINCTIVE ENTERTAINMENT

COCOANUT GROVE

"DESIGNED BY R.O. HODENHORN"

PIEDMONT ST. BOSTON LIBERTY 3256

See the Rolling Roof Dine & Dance under the Stars and Sky

Theatregoer's Dinner $1.50 5 to 9 P.M. Never a Cover Charge

Dancing 6:30 P.M. to 2 A.M.

Floor Shows Twice Nightly 7:30 and 11:30 P.M.

Matchbooks from the Cocoanut Grove, c. 1940.

Found in the debris at the Cocoanut Grove were these shoes and music sheets from the bandleader Micky Alpert, who died in the fire. The title of the song—"Just as Though You Were Here."

Revere Beach

"Love in the forties—you went to Revere Beach
with your date, and you held each other's
hands, and you walked along the shore,
squeezing each other's hands.
That was love."

—Ray Barron

Crescent Beach Station, c. 1900, waiting to take the Narrow Gauge across the Pines/Saugus River. Built in 1896, Revere Beach was a first in America, "the first [beach] that I know of," according to its designer, Charles Eliot, "to be set aside and governed by a public body for the enjoyment of the common people."

The latest Revere Beach fashion in bathing attire, c. 1920.

Previous page: Peek-a-Boo Girls on Revere Beach, 1917. One-piece bathing suits became the rage at the beach after 1906, when an Australian girl was arrested for wearing one.

FROM THE TIME IT OPENED in 1896 until 1940, Revere Beach had easy access from Boston. Electric train service was advertised as a "ferry trip across the harbor, train ride along the shore." For a dime, you would leave the ferry terminal along Atlantic Avenue at Rowes Wharf, cross the harbor, then board the train at Jeffries Point in East Boston. From there you'd travel along the shoreline, with stops at Crescent Beach, Bath House, or Oak Island. Or you could get to the Lynn Station on Market Street and take the beloved "Narrow Gauge" across the Pines/Saugus River. While you sat in one of the plush green or straw seats, the train would hang over the narrow track, making just the water visible below. While sea breezes gently blew through the open windows, thoughts of riding the Cyclone or the taste of an A'Hearn's frozen custard whetted your appetite for fun.

But Revere Beach was much more than an amusement park. There were ocean pier baths—private pools filled with warm, filtered ocean water. A single bath went for $1.25, and, of course, they were separate for men and women. There was dancing at "the casino," the nautical garden, and the renowned Condits Ballroom. This luxurious dance hall hosted many a talented musician of the day, from Rudy Vallee to Woody Herman. The Revere Golden Slipper marathon attracted dancers from all over the country. Then there were the freak shows, the fun house (called the Pit), the bicycle races around the Revere cycle track, and Carver's inimitable diving horses, which would dive from a platform forty feet in the air with their lady riders onboard, into a tank on the beach!

The beach curved for miles along the shore, providing a salty playground for the thousands who flocked there daily. As late as 1933, the beach had strict rules about bathing suits. The local newspaper wrote, "One unforgiveable sin will be dropping the shoulder straps. In proper suits the practice of exposing the back will not be interfered with. But the front must be thoroughly and modestly covered at all times."

Covering up was easy to enforce if you were one of the many who rented a woolen bathing suit at the Revere Bath House. These one-piece suits, which were rented out for a quarter an hour, had scoop fronts and backs with trunks that went down to the knees. The large white clock that faced the ocean told you when it was time to return your suit.

During the war Revere Beach closed at dusk, for fear that the lights of the amusements could be seen by any U-boats that might be in the harbor. It also became a favorite spot for soldiers home on leave. Many an engagement was decided on the shores of the beach, with the sounds of Tommy Dorsey drifting across the water.

Like other old neighborhoods, Revere Beach was lost to the wrecking ball in the 1970s. When sterile condominiums went up, all that remained were the memories. Revere Beach had allowed young and old to enjoy life a bit, to forget about the Depression or the war or the job that wasn't enough to live on. It gave families and young couples just starting out a place to escape the city. With its passing, much more than buildings was lost. Simple times were lost, too, times that allowed people to come together and celebrate the joys of summer.

Bathers, c. 1920. Men had to cover up almost as much as women. Trunks only were not permitted at Revere Beach until the late 1930s.

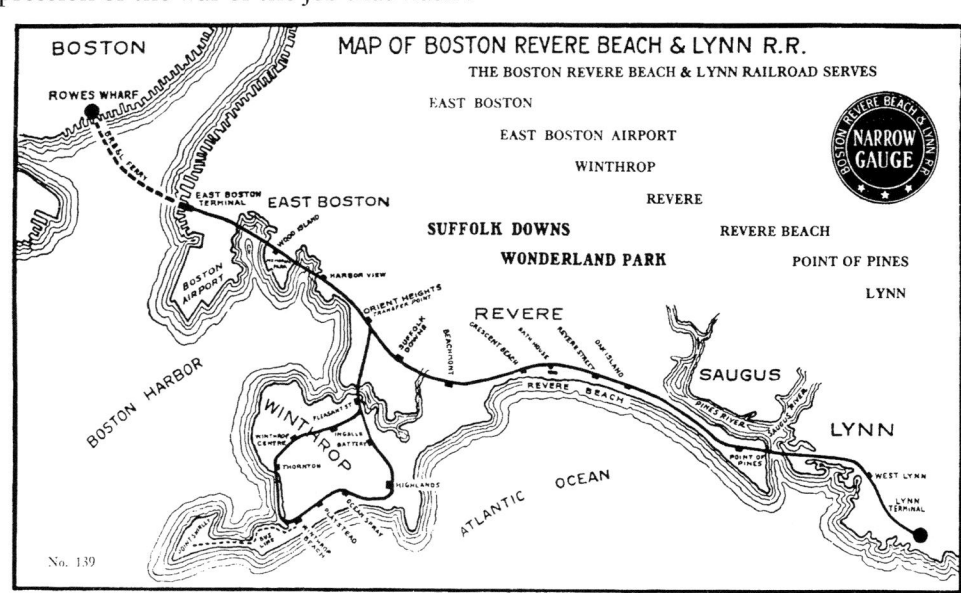

Bostonians could reach Revere Beach by a combination of ferry and narrow-gauge railway, as shown in this map, c. 1920.

The Derby Racer, c. 1920. A double coaster, and one of the original roller coasters at Revere Beach, it thrilled thousands.

Bluebeard's Castle, c. 1940. A landmark at the beach, this was the entryway to the fun house.

"*The greatest thing they had was Nickel Day, that's what we lived for.*"

—Dorothea James
former Revere resident

Above: An ad for Darkness and Dawn, c. 1903, an attraction conducted in the spirit of Dante's Inferno. The visitor would be greeted with devilish spirits and illusions of the depths of hell. Admission, a mere ten cents.

Right: A ride like this would cost twenty-five cents, except during the Depression, when Nickel Days began.

"It was a great way to pass the evening. As a youngster, you passed by the dance halls and heard the bands and the beautiful music coming out."

—Peter McCauley
Revere resident and historian

Above: An ad for the Diving Girls, c. 1910. Between diving horses and diving girls, the beach was never without amusement.

Left: The Ocean Pier. Resplendent out on the boardwalk, this grand building opened in 1911, complete with dining hall and open-air dancing pavilion large enough to hold 2,000 couples. It was said to be without a peer in New England.

Revere Beach bathers, c. 1940. A two-mile stretch of sand and clear waters greeted sun worshippers. Many of the bathing suits seen here were woolen and rented for twenty-five cents an hour.

The Cyclone, mid-1950s. Built in the 1920s, at a cost of $125,000, this ride had a hundred-foot vertical drop, with the trains going as fast as forty-five miles per hour. This Cyclone was said to be faster than its counterparts at Coney Island or Palisades Park.

Mary A'Hearn's frozen custard, c. 1940. Fresh
fruit and cream made up this cooling specialty.

The Braves!

"Everybody loved the Braves."
—George Altison
former Knot Hole Gang member

The Braves 1947 Sketch Book. After the 1948 World Series, the Braves' owner, Lou Perini, said about the team's manager, "Miracle manager my eye. Billy Southworth gets the credit we deserve."

Previous page: Babe Ruth and Wally Berger, 1935. The Sultan of Swat ended his career with over 700 home runs, while Berger set a record for most home runs by a rookie.

SIXTY YEARS AGO, Braves Field was known as the Beehive, and the team was called, what else? the Bees. If that sounds hard to believe, how about the time they were called the Beaneaters? No, the field was not called the Pot, but the managers did state publicly, "This team is a horror show," and proceeded to rename it something less outrageous.

Since baseball began in 1871, it has given cities a great distraction. The Braves, the "other team" in Boston, gave fans something else—a way to divide their loyalties against the Red Sox.

In 1920, shortly after moving to Braves Field, known affectionately as the Wigwam, the team set a record for number of innings played, twenty-six, against the Brooklyn Robins. It still stands today. In 1929 they set another record, coming in dead last in the league and losing ninety-eight games.

Hiring Wally Berger in 1930 was a start at turning the losing team around. In his rookie season under Manager Bill McKechnie, Berger hit thirty-eight home runs. Three years later, with the Braves in the first division for the first time since 1921, a half million fans visited the Wigwam. The players took home a bonus that season of $242 each. But by 1935, with the country deep into the Depression, the franchise was close to bankruptcy. Its owner, Judge Emil Fuchs, needed something to bring the fans back in. His idea of building a dog-racing track in the outfield to raise extra cash was quickly vetoed by the National League. So he did the next best thing, or so he thought, hiring the greatest ballplayer of all time, Babe Ruth.

Coming to Boston completed the circle for the Sultan of Swat. He had begun his career here with the Red Sox in 1914. But returning to play with the Braves twenty-one years later, after hitting his 700th home run, proved too much. Enticed with an offer to replace Manager Bill McKechnie, Ruth approached home plate on Opening Day with a dream even he couldn't deliver. By June the publicity stunt had backfired. Having difficulty rounding the bases and hearing that Casey Stengel, not himself, would be the new manager of the Braves, the mighty Babe laid down his bat.

From 1942 to 1945, the team was filled with rookies as nearly 500 players were called into active military duty. After the war, the pitchers Johnny Sain and Warren Spahn were recruited, and Manager Billy Southworth came aboard from the St. Louis Cardinals. During his first season with the team, Southworth imposed a midnight curfew and strict practice codes, bringing order to the clubhouse. His discipline paid off. The 1948 team was ready to go all the way. During that year's World Series against the Cleveland Indians, the Braves had some of the best players the sport had to offer. Sain, Spahn, Tommy Holmes, Earl Torgeson, and Eddie Stanky put many a run on the scoreboard. But in the end Cleveland's pitching was even better than that of the dynamic duo of Spahn and Sain. The Braves lost the series 4–2, in a six-game showdown.

Warren Spahn said a few years later, "The 1948 team was a conglomeration of experienced players in the twilight of their careers. It was strictly a one-shot proposition." Without a winning team, Boston could not support two national baseball teams. And so in 1953 the Braves were sold to Milwaukee. This time no publicity stunt would bring the fans back to the Wigwam. But despite the losses, Braves Field was a special place with fans who never forgot the team.

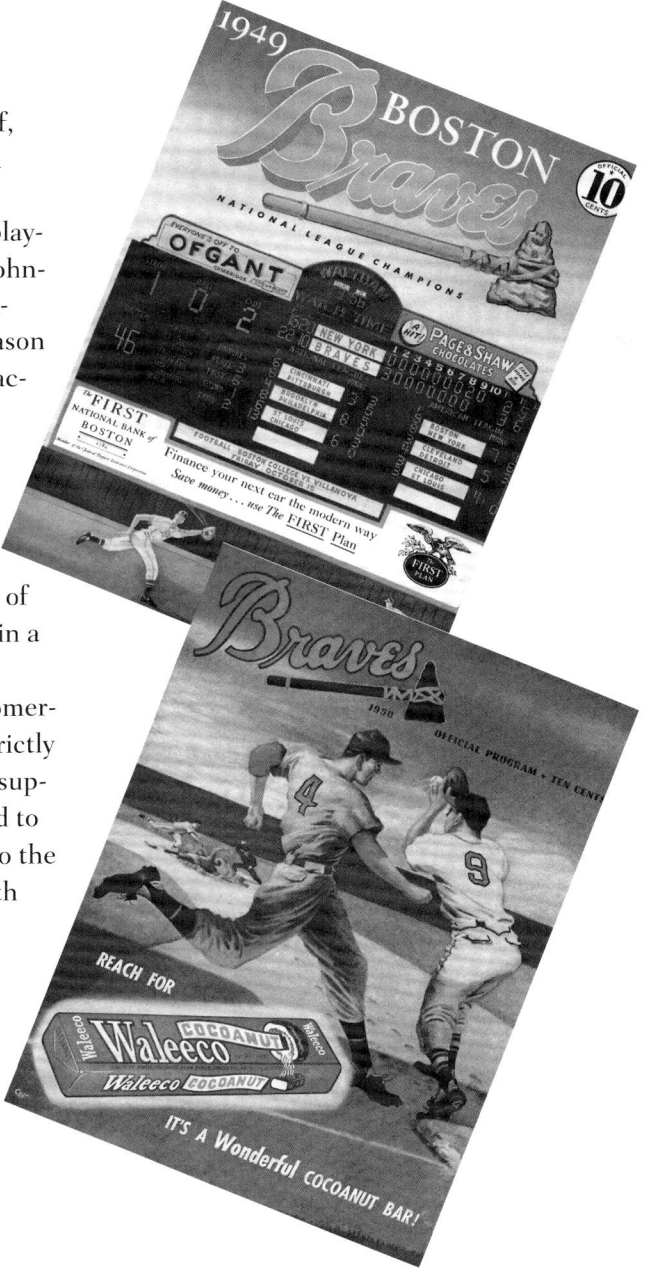

Above: A 1949 Braves program.

Below: A 1950 Braves program. The end of an era for the Boston Braves: after the loss of the 1948 World Series to Cleveland, the team was characterized in a *Globe* editorial as "an old club, crabby, bitter, set in their ways."

MEMBERSHIP CARD Letters and No. YS-44

BRAVES KNOT HOLE GANG

George Altison

is a regular member of the Braves Knot Hole Gang and has subscribed to the agreement on the back of this card.

Agency Somerville Y.M.C.A.

HUNTINGTON R. HARDWICK
Chairman Executive Committee

W. A. MacCORMICK
Executive Secretary

ALWAYS TAKE THIS CARD TO THE GAME

AGREEMENT OF MEMBERSHIP in the
BRAVES KNOT HOLE GANG

1. I will not at any time skip school to attend a game.
2. I will attend no game against the wishes of parents or employer.
3. I will uphold the principles of clean speech, clean sports, and clean habits.
4. I agree to conduct myself as a fair sportsman at all times towards umpires, players, and spectators, and to refrain from cigarettes and profane language on the field.
5. I agree to respect and comply with the rules and regulations of the Boston National League Base Ball Company.
6. I agree to use my membership card personally, and to forfeit it for any violations of the above agreement.

George Altison
Boy's Signature

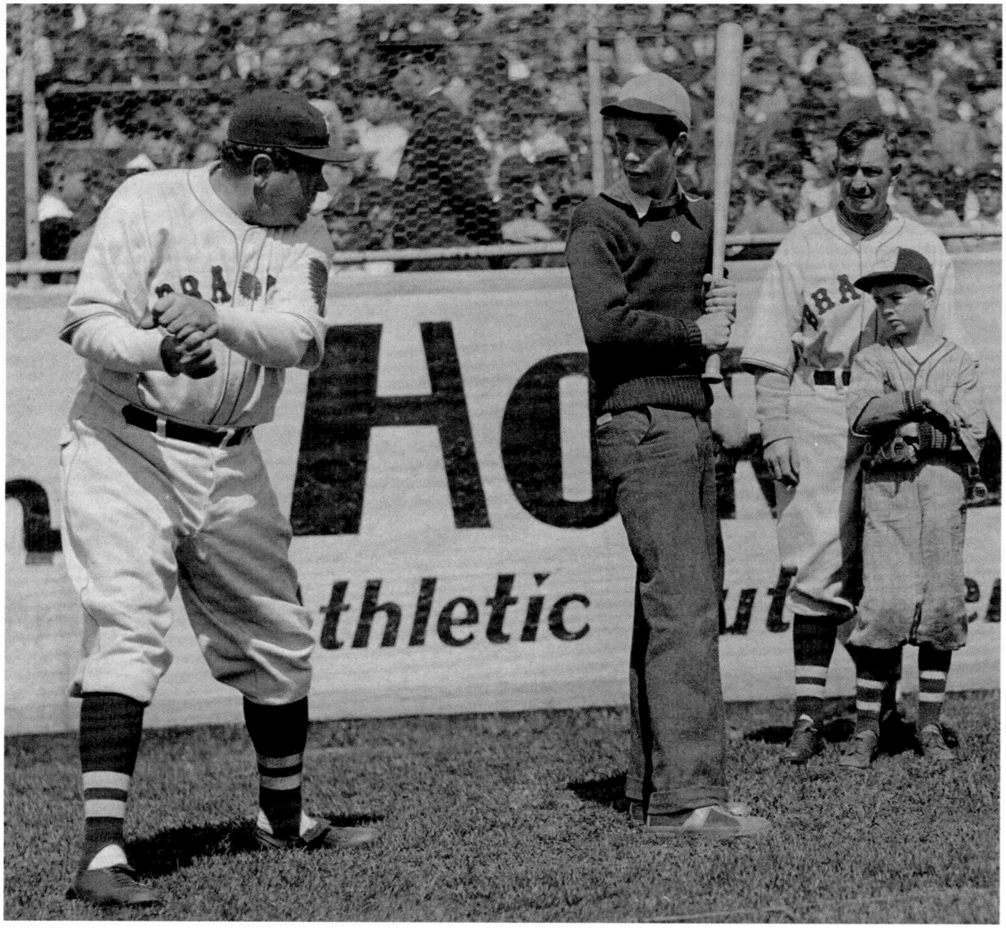

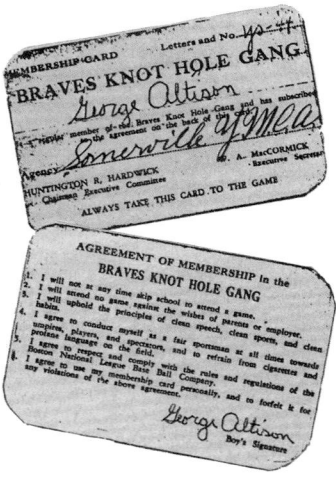

Babe Ruth gives batting tips to the Knot Hole Gang, a club that cost a dollar and gave kids admission to the park all season. Over 25,000 fans came to the Wigwam on Opening Day in 1935 to see Babe Ruth play in a Braves uniform. He hit an RBI single in the first inning and a two-run homer in the fifth, giving the Braves a 4–2 victory.

Aerial view of Braves Field, 1946. Bordered by Commonwealth Ave. and what is now the Mass. Turnpike, the field had a view of the Charles.

Braves Field, c. 1940. During the war years, the Braves had as much trouble filling the roster with talented players as they did filling the Wigwam. By the summer of 1944, they drew the lowest number of fans in either league. But the owner, Lou Perini, predicted that a turnaround was near.

"*Lolly would come armed with Tootsie Rolls and would throw them out to the visiting teams.*"

—Adacie Fox Allen
longtime Braves fan

Lolly Hopkins, a grandmother from Providence, R.I., and her megaphone, c. 1940.

FACING PAGE

Left: The sixth World Series game, Braves vs. Cleveland Indians, 1948. Cleveland Center Fielder Thurman Tucker stumbles toward home plate as Catcher Bill Salkeld of Boston sidesteps him after making the out in an eighth-inning rundown.

Center: Eddie Stanky races for first base in the seventh inning of the final game. Umpire Bill Stewart calls him out. Cleveland went on to win, 4–3, clinching the series four games to two.

Right: Boston Shortstop Alvin Dark looks to the umpire as he slides back into first base too late to keep from being doubled off in the first inning of the final game. Eddie Robinson, the Cleveland first baseman, already has the ball.

Johnny Sain, pitcher, 1948. The right-hander Sain and his teammate Warren Spahn, a lefty, won 153 games between 1947 and 1950. Their 46 percent reliability record gave rise to the phrase "Spahn and Sain, then pray for rain."

Crowd leaving Braves Field, c. 1945. Standing in its place today is Boston University's Nickerson Field. Because of Braves Field's close proximity to the Charles River, it was said if the winds were right, swimmers could catch a fly ball as they stood on Magazine Beach in Cambridge, across the river.

Epilogue

It seems that whenever we look back, we tend to put on rose-colored glasses, making what was "then" seem better than what is "now." That was certainly the case with the era discussed in this book. Everyone I spoke with, for both the television series and the book, would, when asked, gently smile, then begin to remember: first a name, then maybe a place or a song. Reminiscing seemed to transform people, to take them back to the neighborhood or dance floor where they had enjoyed their youth. Maybe that's the reason they remember these things so fondly, because during this era they were younger and things did seem simpler. That's not to say they weren't; it's just that today will probably seem simple to my young son forty to fifty years from now. Perhaps it's our youth and innocence that we miss more than anything else. The songs and the places are just reminders. And each generation has its own unique way of remembering "the way it was."

Index

Colophon

BOSTON: THE WAY IT WAS
was designed, composed, and produced by Scott-Martin Kosofsky at the
Philidor Company, Boston. The text
and quotation typefaces, Fairfield and
an unnamed informal script, are two
designs for metal Linotype by Rudolph
Ruzicka, a Czech-born artist who settled
in Boston in the 1920s. The titling type is
Runic, a late 19th-century "Latin" face.

The photographs were scanned at
Aurora Graphics in Portsmouth, New
Hampshire, which also produced the
final page films. Mr. Kosofsky restored
the damaged images in Adobe Photo-
shop 3.0.4. The book was assembled
entirely on a Macintosh computer
using Quark XPress 3.31.

We are grateful to the lenders for
allowing us access to many of the earliest surviving prints and negatives, and to
Sal Lopes, of Boston, for a number of
superb silver prints.

The book was printed and bound by
Nimrod Press, Westwood, Massachu-
setts. The paper is Westvaco Sterling
Satin, an acid-free sheet.

Picture Credits

Photographs by Leslie Jones, Courtesy of the Boston Public Library Print
Department, except the following: pp. i, vii, viii (bottom), x, xi, 27, 28, 30, 33,
37, 38, 39 (bottom), 40, 41, 42, 43, 45, 46, 53, 58, 59, 60, 61, 65, 85, 95, 117, 118:
Courtesy of the Boston Public Library, Print Department; pp. v, ix (bottom),
3 (both), 5, 7, 15, 18 (bottom), 19 (both), 21, 25, 36, 66, 77 (bottom), 117: Jules
Aarons Collection—Courtesy of The Bostonian Society/Old State House; pp.
viii (top), 10, 12, 17, 22, 23, 24, 35, 67: Jules Aarons; p. 2 (bottom): Courtesy of
the Society for the Preservation of New England Antiquities; pp. 9, 13, 61, 62,
73: Courtesy of The Bostonian Society/Old State House; p. 14: Calvin Camp-
bell, Courtesy of the Boston Public Library Print Department; pp. 18 (top), 20:
Courtesy of Mario Manzelli—The Bostonian Society/Old State House; p. 29:
Fairfield Studio, Courtesy of the Boston Public Library Print Department;
p. 31: Boston Housing Authority; pp. 48 (top), 92 (both), 93 (left): Ray Barron;
p. 54: Photo by Arthur Griffin—then photographer of *The Boston Globe* ; p. 68:
Photo by Proctor, Courtesy of The Bostonian Society/Old State House; pp. 70,
74: © Randolph Langenbach; pp. 72, 93 (right): William J. "Sonny" Jones;
pp. 77 (top), 78 (right), 79 (left): Richard Johnson; pp. 76 (both), 79 (right):
Boston Garden Collection of the Boston Public Library; pp. 78 (left), 84, 107,
108, 109 (both), 110 (left), 111, 114 (all): The Sports Museum of New England;
p. 87: With the permission of Thelma S. Marcus; pp. 88 (both), 94 (bottom), 95
(right): From the collection of Rudy and Barbara Franchi; pp. 89 (middle),
90 (both), 91 (bottom): Bob Pollock; p. 91 (top): Steve Plimpton photo, courtesy
of Bob Bachelder; pp. 94 (top), 95 (left): *Boston Herald* Photo; p. 89 (top):
The Family of Norton D. Clark; pp. 98 (top), 99 (top), 101–106: Peter McCauley
Collection; p. 100: Photo by Leon Abdalian, Courtesy of the Boston Public
Library Print Department; pp. 110 (right), 112, 113 (left): George Altison.